3002300057049X

W9-CKL-975

Karl and Carolina Uncover the Parts of a Book

by Sandy Donovan   illustrated by Michael Mullan

PICTURE WINDOW BOOKS
a capstone imprint

Thanks to our advisers for their expertise, research, and advice:

Diane R. Chen, Library Information Specialist
John F. Kennedy Middle School, Nashville, Tennessee

Terry Flaherty, Ph.D., Professor of English
Minnesota State University, Mankato

Editors: Shelly Lyons and Jennifer Besel
Designer: Abbey Fitzgerald
Art Director: Nathan Gassman
Page Production: Jane Klenk
The illustrations in this book were created digitally.

Picture Window Books
1710 Roe Crest Drive
North Mankato, MN 56003
877-845-8392
www.capstonepub.com

Printed in the United States of America in North Mankato, Minnesota.
042013
007300R

All books published by Picture Window Books
are manufactured with paper containing at least
10 percent post-consumer waste.

Library of Congress Cataloging-in-Publication Data
Donovan, Sandra, 1967–
Karl and Carolina uncover the parts of a book / by Sandy Donovan ;
illustrated by Michael Mullan.
p. cm. — (In the library)
Includes index.
ISBN 978-1-4048-5760-5 (library binding)
ISBN 978-1-4048-6107-7 (paperback)
1. Books—Juvenile literature. I. Mullan, Michael, ill. II. Title.
Z116.A2D65 2010
002—dc22   2009030070

Karl and Carolina are best friends. They do everything together, such as skateboarding and playing chess. And they like many of the same things, such as bananas and funny movies.

Karl and Carolina also love to learn. This week they've learned some new words, a skateboard trick, and how to burp the alphabet. Today they are at the library. They want to learn about dinosaurs.

"This might be a good book," Carolina told Karl.

"How can you tell?" asked Karl. "You haven't even taken it off the shelf."

"You can tell a lot about a book by looking at the spine," said Carolina.

"Spine?" asked Karl. "What's that, like a backbone?"

"Kind of," Carolina answered.

"It's the **edge** of the book. Pages are attached to the inside of the spine. On the outside of the spine, you can find important information about the book. See? Here's the author's last name, the title, and the name of the publisher."

author's last name

title

publisher

call number

Writer
T-Rex and His Friends
LAVA PRESS
567.9
Wri

A library book also has a label on the spine. The label shows the book's call number. A call number is a combination of numbers that tells where the book is shelved in the library.

"So what's the title?"
asked Karl.

Carolina said,

"T-Rex and His Friends."

"That sounds
good," said Karl.
"Hey, how do you
know so much
about spines?"

Writer

T-Rex
and His Friends

LAVA
PRESS

567.9
Wri

"I learned about all the parts of a book at school," Carolina answered.

She pulled the book off the shelf and showed Karl the **cover**.

"On the cover, you can find the title and the author's name. You can also find the illustrator's name, if there is one. This book has one."

"Most covers have a cool drawing or picture of something to make the book look good, right?" asked Karl.

"Right," said Carolina.

"**What are some other parts of a book?**" asked Karl.

Carolina opened the book. "Well," she said, "there's the **title page**. That's the first page of the book. Like the cover, it tells you the title and the full names of the author and the illustrator. It also tells you the publisher."

T-Rex

and His
Friends

by Guy Writer

Then Carolina flipped over the title page and showed Karl what was on the other side.

Lava Press
4875 Jurrasic Ave.
Acacia Lake, TX 78520

"This is the **copyright page**," she said. "This page has all kinds of information on it. The copyright information tells you the year the copyright was given and who owns it. In 2010, Guy Writer claimed the right for this book.

"The text here also tells us

no one can make copies of this book

unless Guy Writer and the publisher give their permission."

"The copyright page also includes Library of Congress Cataloging-in-Publication Data," said Carolina.

"Cata-wa-huh?" asked Karl.

"Nice try," Carolina said. "You can call it 'CIP data' for short. CIP data helps librarians keep track of all the books in their libraries."

You can find the publisher's address on the copyright page, too. If you want to find out more about the book, you can contact the publisher at the address listed. You can also ask for permission to use part of the book on a Web site, in your own book, or somewhere else.

Across from the copyright page was the dedication. Carolina showed it to Karl.

To Mom, who taught me to dig dinos.

Guy Writer

"A **dedication** is a special message from the author," she said. "Sometimes the author thanks or honors somebody by dedicating the book to that person. Guy Writer dedicated this book to his mom. Isn't that sweet?"

"He should have dedicated it to dinosaurs," said Karl.

On the next two pages, they found the book's **table of contents**. Carolina said, "This is a list of the book's chapters and the page number on which each chapter begins. The table of contents helps readers quickly see what information is in the book. It also helps readers easily find things in the book."

"Kind of like a map of the book?" Karl asked.

"Exactly," said Carolina.

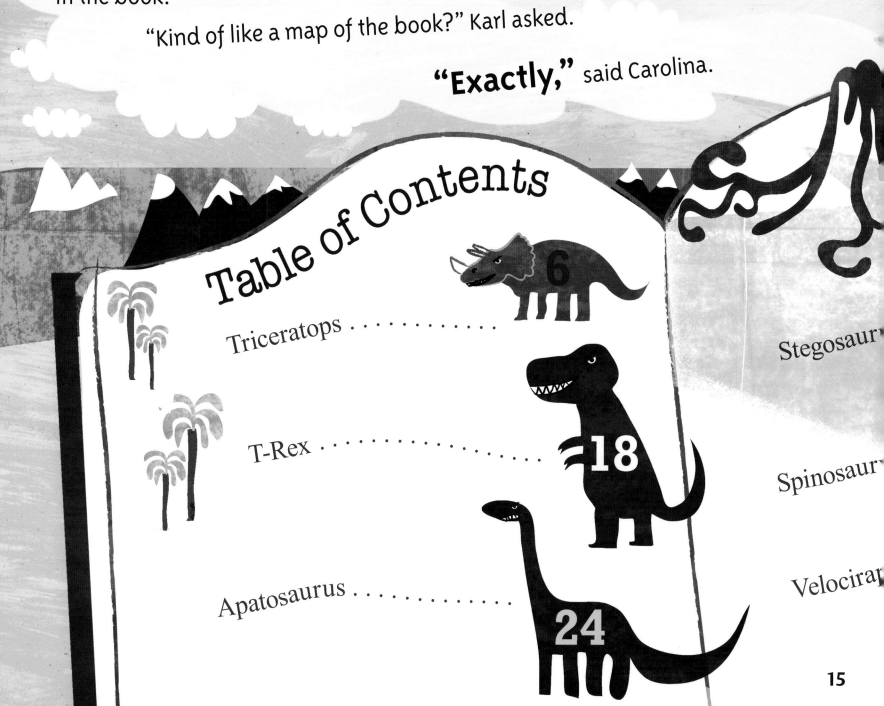

Table of Contents

Carolina turned the page again.

Karl said, **"Ah-ha**! This looks like the good part of the book."

Triceratops was an herbivore. It had a parrot-like beak and three horns on its head. Its head was surrounded by a large bony frill.

"You got it," said Carolina. "This is the **main text**. It's all the words that make up the main part of a book. If the book is fiction, the main text of the book is the story. If the book is nonfiction, like this one, the main text is all the information the author wanted to give. The main text is what readers spend most of their time on."

Tyrannosaurus Rex is also known as T-Rex. It was one ...d huge pointy teeth.

"This is where you really sink your teeth in," Karl said, chomping like a T-Rex.

Before Karl could start to read, Carolina turned to the end of the book.

"At the end of nonfiction books, you'll often find a **glossary** and an **index**. This book has both," she said.

"A glossary is kind of like a tiny dictionary. It lists any difficult or important words from the book and gives a definition for each."

GLOSSARY

carnivore—a meat-eating animal
frill—a bony plate that surrounds the head of some dinosaurs
herbivore—a plant-eating animal
horn—a hard, often curved and pointed, growth found on the heads of some animals, such as dinosaurs and cattle

"The index is different," said Carolina. "That's a list of topics covered in the book. It gives the page numbers where those topics are discussed. One topic in Guy Writer's index is horns. If you wanted to learn more about horns, you could check the index and see on what pages the author talks about them. Cool, right?"

"**Cool**," said Karl.

INDEX

Carolina shut the book. She wanted to show Karl the back cover.

"The **back cover** usually has a summary of the book," she explained.

"From the summary, people can find out what the book is about. The back cover also has a bar code. That's a block of stripes in the lower corner. See how the stripes look kind of like bars? A bookseller can scan the bar code with a computer to get information about the book. A librarian will sometimes add another bar code that's just for that library."

Learn more about T-Rex explores fossil park wit friends in this sharp te

Once the lava party b there is no turning b

The bar code gives a book's ISBN, or International Standard Book Number. The ISBN is a long number that tells a computer a lot about the book, such as who published it and how much it costs. Every book has a different ISBN.

ISBN 978-1-4048-5760-5

90000

"Wow," Karl said. "I never knew there were so many **parts of a book**. Thanks for teaching me!"

"You're welcome," said Carolina. "Come on, let's check out this book so we can learn more about T-Rex!"

"Yeah!" said Karl.

Glossary

bar code—a block of bars found on a book's back cover; librarians and booksellers scan the code to find out information about the book.

CIP data—stands for Cataloging-in-Publication Data; the information from the Library of Congress that lists the author, the illustrator, a short summary of the book, and the ISBN.

copyright—the right to publish something

copyright page—a page near the front of a book that gives information about who owns the rights to the contents of the book; also called the verso page.

cover—the thick outer layer of a book; the cover has a front and back.

dedication—a message from the author about the book, usually thanking or honoring someone

fiction—books that are made-up stories written by an author

glossary—a list of words used in a book, along with their definitions

illustrator—the person who makes the drawings in a book

index—a list of topics covered in a nonfiction book, along with the page numbers on which they are discussed

ISBN—a 10- or 13-digit number that identifies a particular title and edition of a book; it stands for International Standard Book Number.

main text—the words that fill up most of the pages of a book; the words the author wrote.

nonfiction—books that are written by an author with the purpose of teaching something

publisher—the company or person who makes a book, magazine, or other piece of work

spine—the part of a book's cover that's on the edge; pages are attached to the inside of the spine, and information about the book is printed on the outside.

table of contents—the page in a book that lists what is found in the main text

title page—the first printed page inside a book; usually it says the title of the book, the author's name, illustrator's name, and publisher's name.

More Books to Read

Berg, Brook. *When Marion Copied: Learning About Plagiarism*. Fort Atkinson, Wis.: Upstart Books, 2006.

Buzzeo, Toni. *Our Librarian Won't Tell Us Anything*. Fort Atkinson, Wis.: Upstart Books, 2006.

Kirk, Daniel. *Library Mouse*. New York: Abrams Books for Young Readers, 2007.

Morris, Carla D. *The Boy Who Was Raised by Librarians*. Atlanta: Peachtree, 2007.

Internet Sites

FactHound offers a safe, fun way to find Internet sites related to this book. All of the sites on FactHound have been researched by our staff.

Here's all you do:

Visit *www.facthound.com*

FactHound will fetch the best sites for you!

Index

Look for all the books in the In the Library series:

Bob the Alien Discovers the Dewey Decimal System

Bored Bella Learns About Fiction and Nonfiction

Karl and Carolina Uncover the Parts of a Book

Pingpong Perry Experiences How a Book Is Made